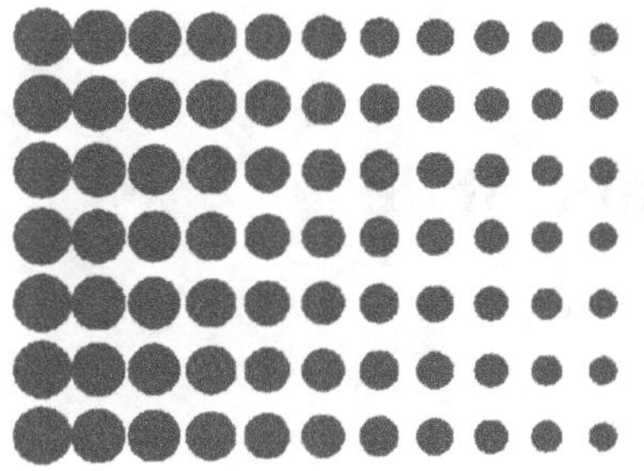

DISCOVER YOUR PSYCHOLOGICAL TYPE

Ray Laferla, Ph.D.

Also by Ray Laferla:

Discover Your Management Style

©RA Laferla, Ph.D., 2016

First published 2001.
Revised and Reprinted 2002.
ISBN: 0-620-28235-5

Corporate and Human Development Specialists

Acknowledgements

I would like to acknowledge the following people, each of whom has made a major contribution to this publication:

- Jeanette Laferla, my wife, whose continued support enables me to carry out the work that I am called to do. Jeanette also gave instinctively of herself in editing the manuscript and challenging me to think through issues;

- Pat Sullivan, my good friend and mentor, who generously gave of his time and talents to expertly edit this work; and

- the many participants in my seminars and workshops who willingly responded to the PTI Questionnaire, giving me the crucial feedback I needed to validate the instrument.

Table of Contents

Table of Contents (continued)

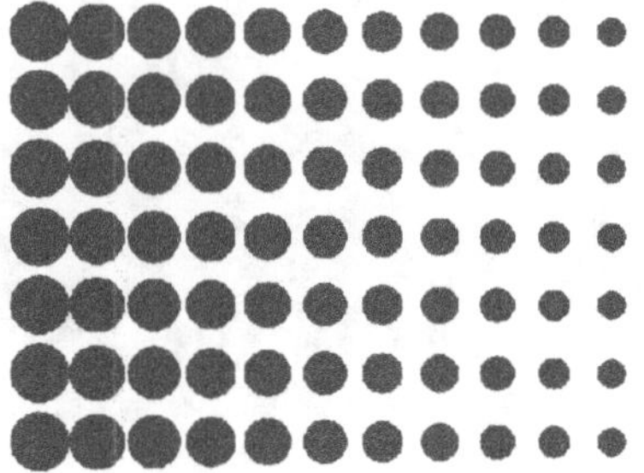

1
Understanding
Psychological
Type

Understanding Psychological Type

What is "Psychological Type"?

Psychological Type is based on the idea that people have preferences. At a simple level everyone knows that some people are right-handed and others are left-handed. Some people like to exercise, others would rather not; some people enjoy being alone whilst others prefer to engage in activities involving others, and so on.

Psychological preferences focus on the fact that people are predisposed to interact with others and the world in different ways. For example, some people make decisions based on how they feel, whereas others make decisions on rational factors.

The key point to remember is that psychological type deals with psychological *preferences only*. It has nothing to do with what may be right or wrong. It also has nothing to do with competencies. It is, therefore, not judgemental in any way.

The four dimensions

We will be examining psychological type in terms of four dimensions:

- how you prefer to be energised;
- how you prefer to gather information;
- how you prefer to make decisions; and
- which lifestyle you prefer to adopt.

Everyone is different

It is important to remember that we are limiting ourselves to four dimensions, and from these dimensions we will identify common traits of people who share certain preferences.

People with common traits tend to be similar in their natures. However, notwithstanding their similarities, everyone is different because there are many more than four dimensions to a person. So, although people with the same preferences may act in similar ways, they are also different in other ways.

The origins of psychological type

Psychological type originated with the work of Swiss psychiatrist Carl Jung, who published his work in a book called "Psychological Types" in 1921.

Two women from the USA, Katherine Briggs and her daughter Isabel Myers, expanded on Jung's theory and developed an instrument called the "Myers-Briggs Type Indicator (MBTI)", which is today the most widely used psychological inventory in the world.

The "Energising" dimension   The first of the four scales is called the "Energising" scale and comprises two polarities called "Introversion" and "Extroversion". This scale has to do with the focusing of attention and how people are energised (i.e. what charges or stimulates them). It is, therefore, called the Energising scale.

This may be illustrated as follows:

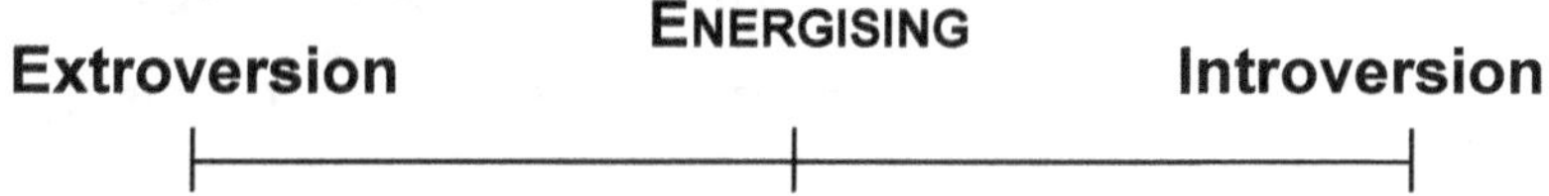

People who prefer *Extroversion* focus on the outer world of people and the environment. They are energised by activity and experience.

On the other hand, those who prefer *Introversion* focus more on their inner world. They like to reflect, and are energised by having the space and time to contemplate.

The "Information-gathering" dimension   The information-gathering dimension has to do with the way in which people acquire data. The names given to the opposite preferences on this scale are *"Sensing"* and *"Intuition"*, namely:

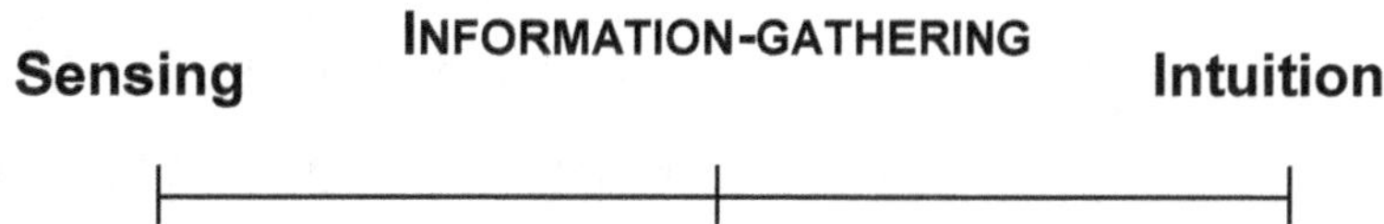

One way people gather information is through the use of their senses. Their eyes, ears and other senses tell them what is there. *Sensing* people prefer to use their senses for establishing facts and interpreting the realities of a situation. They tend to be detail oriented and are realistic and practical.

The other way to deal with information is through *Intuition.* Intuitive people seek meanings and possibilities that go beyond what is directly available to the senses. Intuitive types value imagination and inspiration.

The "Decision-making" dimension

Having acquired information either intuitively or through the senses, decisions need to be made. The opposites on the decision-making scale are *"Thinking"* and *"Feeling"*:

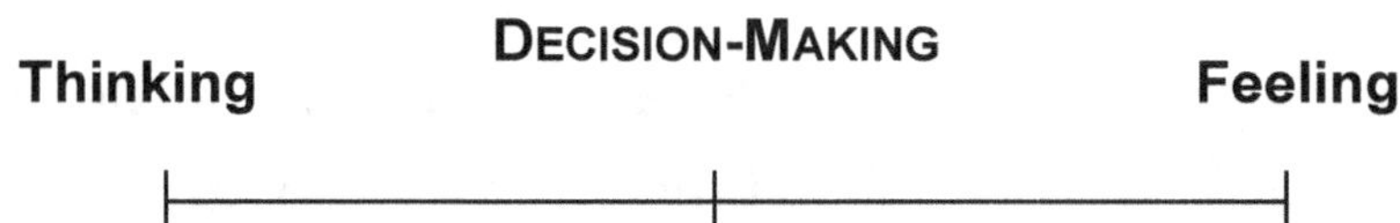

People who prefer to logically weigh up the evidence to come to an objective decision are employing the *Thinking* function. Such types are usually good at analysing and diagnosing what is wrong with something.

The opposite preference to *Thinking* is *Feeling.* *Feeling* people prefer to make decisions based on how much they care and what appeals to them. Personal values are paramount. It is important to understand that the term *"Feeling"* does not refer to emotions but to values.

The "Lifestyle" dimension

This last dimension describes the lifestyle people prefer to adopt when dealing with issues. The opposites on this scale are *"Judging"* and *"Perceiving"*:

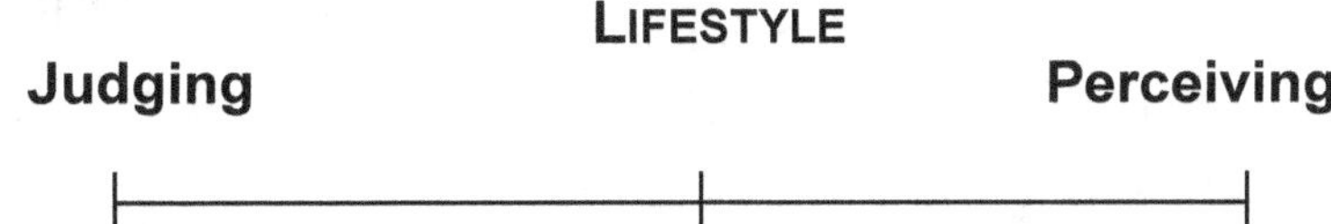

Those who prefer the *Judging* attitude tend to live in a planned, orderly way. They like to be in control of matters and they organise themselves in a structured manner. (The word "structured" defines this preference quite well.)

The other lifestyle preference is one characterised by flexibility. Thus, *Perceiving* people prefer to live in a spontaneous, flexible manner. They like to keep their options open and adapt to each situation as it comes up. They also seek to understand life rather than control it.

__Eight possible preferences__   Because each of the four dimensions have a scale with two opposite attributes, eight preferences are rated when evaluating psychological type.

These are:

Extroversion / Introversion
Sensing / Intuition
Thinking / Feeling
Judging / Perceiving

These preferences are given the following initials:

E = Extroversion

I = Introversion

S = Sensing

N = Intuition · (the letter "I" has already been allocated to Introversion so the next letter in the name I<u>n</u>tuition is used)

T = Thinking

F = Feeling

J = Judging

P = Perceiving

Sixteen possible psychological types

With eight preferences we have sixteen possible combinations of Psychological Type:

ESTJ	ENTJ	ISTP	INTP
ESFJ	ENFJ	ISFP	INFP
ESTP	ESFP	ISTJ	ISFJ
ENTP	ENFP	INTJ	INFJ

Your particular Psychological Type (i.e. which one of the sixteen combinations applies to you) may be established by responding to the questionnaire that follows.

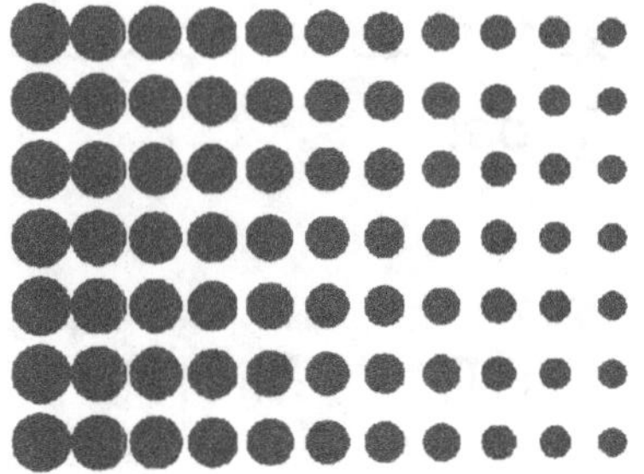

2
Psychological
Type Inventory

Psychological Type Inventory

Instructions

To establish your Psychological Type you are required to respond to sixty questions.

Choose either *x* or *y* for each question and annotate the appropriate block with a tick ✓. When you have finished, transfer your responses to the Scoring Sheet on page 31. Each question must be answered. Please note that there are no right or wrong answers, only preferences.

1. When waiting in line do you usually:

    x ☐ talk with others; or

    y ☐ keep to yourself?

2. Do you find people who come up with radical, unconventional ideas:

    x ☐ rather annoying; or

    y ☐ quite fascinating?

3.   If you are required to address an unpleasant issue with someone, are you likely to be:

x ☐ direct and frank; or

y ☐ tactful and considerate?

4.   Do you generally:

x ☐ do things well in advance; or are you

y ☐ inclined to procrastinate?

5.   Would you describe yourself as more:

x ☐ outgoing; or

y ☐ reserved?

6.   When putting something together for the first time, do you:

x ☐ read instructions carefully before assembling it; or

y ☐ scan instructions briefly, then get into action, noticing how things fit as you proceed?

7. Do you consider yourself to be more:

x ☐ tough-minded; or

y ☐ sensitive?

8. Do you:

x ☐ schedule activities carefully; or

y ☐ do things as they come up?

9. When the telephone rings, would you prefer to:

x ☐ answer it yourself; or

y ☐ leave it for someone else to answer?

10. Are you more:

x ☐ practical; or

y ☐ creative?

11. Would you say your decisions are ruled more by your:

x ☐ head; or your

y ☐ heart?

12. Are you more satisfied:

x ☐ when you have completed something; or

y ☐ when you are working on something you enjoy?

13. Which do you think you do most:

x ☐ talk; or

y ☐ listen?

14. Is it worse to:

x ☐ live in a make-believe world; or

y ☐ be in a rut?

15. If you were required to interview someone for a job would you be:

     x ☐ objective and impersonal; or

     y ☐ friendly and amiable?

16. In your business dealings, do you prefer to:

     x ☐ have formal contracts drawn up; or

     y ☐ agree things verbally?

17. At a party:

     x ☐ are you one of the last to leave; or

     y ☐ are you one of those who leave at a reasonable time?

18. Which do you consider to be more important:

     x ☐ details; or

     y ☐ principles?

19. Which approach is likely to influence you more:

    x ☐ factual information; or

    y ☐ an emotional appeal?

20. When on holiday do you prefer to:

    x ☐ plan activities; or

    y ☐ act spontaneously?

21. Do you consider yourself to be more of:

    x ☐ an outgoing person; or

    y ☐ a private person?

22. Having learnt something new, do you generally:

    x ☐ apply what you have learnt before learning something new; or

    y ☐ move on to learn something else before fully applying your knowledge?

23. Which declaration do you consider to be more complimentary:

x ☐ "You're a logical person"; or

y ☐ "You're a feeling person"?

24. Given the choice, would you prefer to:

x ☐ do one thing at a time and move from one completed task to the next; or

y ☐ handle a variety of tasks simultaneously?

25. Do you generally:

x ☐ act before you think; or

y ☐ think before you act?

26. Which statement appeals to you more:

x ☐ "Don't change what is working"; or

y ☐ "Continually change to improve even those things that are working"?

27. With your colleagues and co-workers do you:

x ☐ seldom give compliments; or

y ☐ express appreciation often?

28. When facing an important deadline, are you usually:

x ☐ tense and driven to get things done; or

y ☐ relaxed while applying yourself?

29. Do you:

x ☐ like music or activity in the background while you work; or

y ☐ seek quietness to concentrate?

30. When assigned a new project, do you:

x ☐ seek as much detail as possible; or

y ☐ prefer the 'big picture' rather than too much detail?

31. At work, is it more natural for you to:

x ☐ do what you have to do, regardless of what others think; or

y ☐ want to please others?

32. Does it upset you when plans have been formulated and you are required to reschedule your activities?

x ☐ Yes.

y ☐ No.

33. Does interacting with strangers:

x ☐ stimulate you; or

y ☐ drain you?

34. Do you prefer to:

x ☐ work with your hands (practically); or

y ☐ work with your mind (conceptually)?

35. Which will influence you more when making a decision:

x ☐ facts and information; or

y ☐ feelings and desires?

36. Which statement describes you best:

x ☐ having a sense of urgency; or

y ☐ being unhurried or unruffled?

37. At your place of work, are you more inclined to:

x ☐ be sociable and gregarious; or

y ☐ keep to yourself?

38. When listening to an authority speak on his/her subject, do you:

x ☐ expect the speaker to be factual and clear-cut; or

y ☐ prefer metaphors, stories and figurative speech to stimulate thought?

39. When faced with the decision to disclose information that is likely to elicit a strong negative reaction, would you:

x ☐ disclose it, with truth as your primary objective; or

y ☐ withhold it, with harmony your primary objective?

40. Having spent a long time on a project that is nearing its conclusion, are you likely to:

x ☐ finalise things and bring the project to an end even though further information may still be available; or

y ☐ delay completion of the project to incorporate additional information?

41. Do strangers get to know what you think and feel:

x ☐ quite quickly; or

y ☐ only after a while (when you know one another reasonably well)?

42. Are you inclined to focus on:

☐ present, day-to-day realities; or

☐ future possibilities?

43. Would you prefer to have, as a boss, someone who is:

    x ☐ demanding and firm (but fair); or

    y ☐ kind and empathetic?

44. In general, would you prefer to:

    x ☐ make things happen; or

    y ☐ let things happen?

45. Do you have:

    x ☐ a great number of friends and acquaintances; or

    y ☐ few, but deep, friendships?

46. Are you drawn more to:

    x ☐ facts; or

    y ☐ ideas?

47. Would you:

x ☐ readily give people unpleasant feedback if it is warranted; or

y ☐ avoid giving people unpleasant feedback unless you have to?

48. Do you usually:

x ☐ put work before recreation; or

y ☐ give recreation and rest an equal or higher priority than work?

49. Which word describes you better:

x ☐ demonstrative; or

y ☐ shy?

50. Is it more important to be:

x ☐ someone who is grounded in the present; or

y ☐ someone who is an idealistic visionary?

51. When someone dresses or behaves differently from others do you:

- **x** [ ] criticise the person (silently or otherwise); or
- **y** [ ] accept the individual (and maybe even find it rather interesting)?

52. Would you prefer to:

- **x** [ ] have things settled; or
- **y** [ ] keep your options open?

53. Would you find a silent weekend retreat (where you are not allowed to talk):

- **x** [ ] frustrating; or
- **y** [ ] appealing?

54. Which of these words describes you better:

- **x** [ ] cautious; or
- **y** [ ] risk-taker?

55. Which type of intelligence appeals to you more:

x ☐ logical intelligence; or

y ☐ emotional intelligence?

56. Would you describe yourself as more:

x ☐ organised; or

y ☐ flexible?

57. Would you prefer to spend your time:

☐ interacting and socialising with many people; or

☐ with a few people who are close to you?

58. Which of the following statements do you consider to be more valid:

☐ "Success is 90% perspiration and 10% inspiration"; or

☐ "Success is 90% inspiration and 10% perspiration"?

59. Which word appeals to you more:

x ☐ analyse; or

y ☐ empathise?

60. Would you describe yourself as being more:

x ☐ systematic and orderly; or

y ☐ easy-going and adaptable?

Scoring Your Responses

Scoring   To ascertain your Psychological Type, transfer your responses to the *x* or *y* blocks. Then, allocating one point for every ✔, calculate the total for each column. There are eight columns, each denoting a preference.

Now that you have a number for each preference, choose the higher number in each pair and circle the preference (e.g. E or I, S or N, T or F, J or P). You will end up with 4 letters. These letters make up your psychological type.

E / I		S / N		T / F		J / P	
x *y*		*x* *y*		*x* *y*		*x* *y*	
1		2		3		4	
5		6		7		8	
9		10		11		12	
13		14		15		16	
17		18		19		20	
21		22		23		24	
25		26		27		28	
29		30		31		32	
33		34		35		36	
37		38		39		40	
41		42		43		44	
45		46		47		48	
49		50		51		52	
53		54		55		56	
57		58		59		60	

E ☐ ☐ I   S ☐ ☐ N   T ☐ ☐ F   J ☐ ☐ P

Psychological **=** ☐☐☐☐
Type

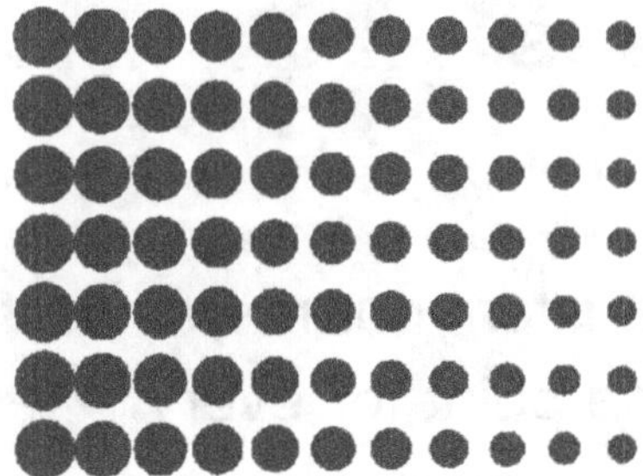

3
Type
Profiles

Type Profiles

ESTJ

In a nutshell

ESTJs are traditionalists who ensure that procedures are adhered to and standards met. They fulfil their obligations dutifully and expect others to do the same. ESTJs are, therefore, somewhat conservative, action-oriented people who roll up their sleeves and get on with things. They are analytical and decisive, and plan their work well in advance.

Words that describe this psychological type are:
- logical;
- systematic;
- efficient;
- practical;
- conscientious;
- tough-minded; and
- well organised.

General characteristics

ESTJs are stable, predictable people who like structure and need things to be orderly. They are not people who are frivolous and they apply themselves to undertaking tasks in a no-nonsense manner.

ESTJs are loyal and considerate. They will go to a great deal of trouble to help family members and friends in need.

ESTJs are worriers. Because they are so diligent they are not at peace until assignments have been completed, their duties done and loose ends tied up.

ESTJs are conservative people who like to stay with the familiar. They are pragmatic people who, though not resistant to change, will ask questions like "Do we need to?", "How will it affect us?" and "Is it practical?" before they commit themselves to a new course of action.

ESTJs are responsible people who can be counted on to follow through with a job. Because they also have a strong sense of duty, they are inclined to take on more work than they can reasonably handle. ESTJs, therefore, need to know that their conscientiousness can be a double-edged sword; on the one hand they get things done and can be relied upon but, on the other hand, they are inclined to overload themselves to the point of exhaustion.

ESTJs learn best in structured situations where objectives have been set, work is mapped out in a logical sequence and they get involved in experiential activities. They are practical people who dislike concepts and theories that are not grounded in utility. ESTJs also find that they need to practise what they learn. So, having been taught something new, they seek to apply it before moving on.

ESTJs put work before play and business before pleasure. For them leisure is earned and must have a purpose. A walk is not just a walk – there is a purpose in it, such as keeping fit, getting to know the countryside, or spending time with somebody else. When ESTJs go on holiday, things must be properly planned and itineraries established. They have a need to make the most of a situation, and feel uncomfortable without structure.

Relationships People, particularly friends and family members, are very important to ESTJs. For this psychological type, relationships are not entered into lightly. When they commit themselves they stay with the relationship and, should it break down, they take it personally.

Because ESTJs are so logical they do not romanticise love. They know that all personal relationships have their ups and downs. So, when things are down, they simply carry on and can even be insensitive to the feelings of their partners.

Counter-productive tendencies ESTJs tend to overuse their strengths to the point that they may become   weaknesses. These people are conscientious but they overdo it; they are decisive but may decide too quickly and overlook important information in their endeavours to come to closure; they are consistent and stay with what they know, but may get themselves into a rut. ESTJs, therefore, need to practise moderation. They need to give themselves enough time to relax without feeling guilty, and act spontaneously from time to time. They also need to deliberately seek change every now and again, simply for a different experience.

ESTJs are so focused on practical issues that they tend to overlook everyday niceties. Under stress they drive themselves particularly hard and may come across as dogmatic and uncaring, often forgetting to express normal pleasantries such as "please" and "thank you".

When important things go wrong, ESTJs tend to blame themselves. In this instance they are likely to become discouraged and extremely negative, to the point that they are uncharacteristically irrational.

ENTJ

In a nutshell   ENTJs are confident, creative people who like to organise events and be in charge. They are assertive, objective and organised. They are also excellent problem solvers.

Words that describe this psychological type are:

- analytical;
- decisive;
- challenging;
- competitive;
- tough-minded;
- strategic thinking; and
- creative.

General characteristics   ENTJs are natural leaders. They use their considerable analytical and reasoning abilities to plan and control as much as they possibly can.

ENTJs believe that conduct should be motivated by logic and they govern their behaviour accordingly. They have definite guiding principles and convictions that dictate their actions and their expectations of others.

ENTJs are creative people. They see possibilities and make connections beyond what is apparent. Consequently, these people take a helicopter view, seeing things from an overall perspective and noticing how facts interlink with one another.

ENTJs are not detail oriented. They quickly become bored with too much routine or detail and need constant stimulation and challenges to keep them motivated. The ideal situation for an ENTJ is to hand over a project once it has reached the maintenance stage and major problems have been overcome. If this is not possible, it becomes a major challenge not to abandon the project before it is completed.

ENTJs take charge quickly and deal decisively with obstacles or problems. They are masters of eliminating confusion and inefficiencies, going to the core of issues, and resolving them with a minimum of fuss.

ENTJs are excellent problem solvers. They are highly analytical, recognising differences between categories and discriminating between the important and unimportant. They quickly decide on the required outcome, and consider creative strategies to achieve it.

ENTJs are good at strategic planning. They look into the future, map out scenarios, establish critical performance requirements and develop action plans to achieve their goals.

ENTJs have a high need for achievement. However, the achievement is not necessarily desired by others. ENTJs set their own standards.

Though their drive and determination are likely to be respected by others, ENTJs need to be aware that these attributes are fuelled by the ever-present, if hidden, fear of failure. Winning is crucial for such a person and the notion that he or she may fail will drive an ENTJ to distraction.

ENTJs, therefore, have difficulty relaxing. For most of them, work is life and life is work. Even when engaged in exercise or recreation, they pit themselves against others and against their own standards of performance.

Relationships   Being extroverted, ENTJs will be energised by interactions with others and will network widely with people.

For ENTJs, however, relationships are a means to an end. People will either support their visions and stimulate their thinking, or the relationship will not be encouraged. ENTJs have no qualms about ending relationships that have outlived their usefulness.

Counter-productive tendencies

As positive and desirable as a decisive and goal-oriented nature is, ENTJs tend to employ these attributes to the point where they become weaknesses. For example, because of the need to achieve and reach closure, they may decide too quickly, overlooking data that may come in late. Also, they are inclined to be impatient when things do not go according to plan. When this happens they tend to over-control.

Because ENTJs are achievement driven they are inclined to overlook niceties such as expressing appreciation and listening to the viewpoints of others. Indeed, they are often judgemental and critical, especially when their high expectations are not met. This can cause staff to become demoralised.

Under stress ENTJs may be overwhelmed by fears of failure and self-doubt. They may feel isolated and unrecognised, unable to reveal their distress to others for fear of appearing weak.

ISTP

In a nutshell ISTPs are logical, sensible people. They enjoy solitude and need time to reflect.

ISTPs are also curious. They are interested in why things happen and how things work. This makes them practical and analytical, excelling at finding working solutions to problems.

Words that describe this psychological type are:

- logical;
- realistic;
- analytical;
- independent thinker;
- adventurous;
- flexible; and
- determined.

General characteristics ISTPs are determined realists who know what they want and who use their reasoning to adapt to situations. They are aware of what is going on around them, and they respond quickly to circumstances to ensure that the chances of success are in their favour. Patience and perseverance come naturally to ISTPs.

ISTPs are independent thinkers. They evaluate facts from a detached perspective and come to their own conclusions. Their decisions are rational, usually based on a great deal of specific information. ISTPs are, therefore, good at solving problems in an analytical and logical manner.

ISTPs are practical, realistic people. They focus on present realities and seldom engage in wishful thinking or theoretical possibilities. They are often good at hands-on activities; most ISTPs are mechanically adept and good at sporting activities.

ISTPs are impatient with inefficiencies. They believe in the easiest and most effective way of addressing and completing tasks. Thus, they do not like to waste effort and will often find new ways of doing things.

ISTPs do not like too many rules. They need some rules, which they regard as guidelines, but are quick to adapt or bend rules if it is in their interests to do so.

ISTPs are egalitarian, believing that all people should be treated fairly and given equal opportunities; they feel that rewards should be in line with one's contribution, and success should be earned.

ISTPs are usually confident. They know what they stand for and, if asked, are quite willing to express their views. Should others disagree with these views, ISTPs are open to hearing different perspectives and will readily adapt a position if facts warrant it.

ISTPs are adventurers; they like new experiences and

are prepared to take reasonable risks. They need variety. Because they have a wide range of interests they need to be presented with projects that challenge them.

The opportunity to pursue their personal interests is important to ISTPs. They commit themselves and will do what it takes to become skilled in their pursuits. ISTPs need to have the right tools to succeed and they will spend as much as they can afford to have the finest equipment available for whatever they want to do.

ISTPs thrive on challenges and novelties. To solve problems and deliver a superb performance is a driving force for them.

Relationships ISTPs are inclined to have a few deep friendships rather than a wide variety of friends. Their relationships generally take a long time to develop as they are reluctant to disclose their views and thoughts until they trust people. However, once ISTPs have committed themselves to others, they will typically stand by them, whatever it takes.

Counter-productive tendencies

ISTPs are inclined to focus so much on keeping things moving that they may ignore the needs and feelings of the people they work and live with.

Because ISTPs are somewhat reserved (introverted) they tend not to share enough information, expecting others to know what they themselves know. When errors are made because of a lack of knowledge, ISTPs become frustrated and express themselves in a critical and direct manner. Such behaviour is often perceived to be insensitive and uncaring.

If ISTPs do not receive recognition for their gifts and talents, and if they are not appreciated for their contributions, they tend to become cynical and negative. In these circumstances they tend to withdraw, and put off making decisions.

ISTPs focus on achieving short-term results rather than looking ahead and planning for the future. When this is overdone they may lose track of the implications of their decisions in the long term.

Under significant stress, the reserved ISTP demonstrates atypical behaviour by erupting in emotional outbursts. This is unnerving to others because it is a departure from the norm. It is also embarrassing for the ISTP, who usually regrets the incident later.

INTP

In a nutshell INTPs are private individuals who enjoy conceptual and scientific pursuits. They enjoy using their intellect to solve problems, which they do in an innovative yet logical manner.

INTPs have clearly defined interests that engage their attention. They dislike small talk or ill-considered views. They also abhor routine and need constant intellectual challenges to stimulate and motivate them.

Words that describe the INTP psychological type are:

- reserved;
- independent thinker;
- conceptual;
- logical;
- sceptical;
- visionary; and
- contemplative.

General characteristics INTPs are mainly concerned with the inner worlds of thoughts and ideas. They use their intellect to analyse issues objectively and in a detached manner, with an ability to pursue goals single-mindedly. Their greatest strength is to logically evaluate situations and establish governing principles.

INTPs are visionaries. They look to the future and see all sorts of possibilities. They also see how things fit with one another and like to create conceptual models.

INTPs are sceptical people. While they are open to new ideas they do not accept conclusions unless their validity can be established.

INTPs have a high need for achievement. However, success is not necessarily measured by the conventional standards of position, status and power. Rather, achievement is reflected in a constant drive for competence and influence, based on knowledge.

INTPs are very critical of themselves and others although, being introverted, they may not express their views to others unless provoked.

INTPs are perpetual students. They need to be given opportunities to learn and, if not, are likely to create learning occasions.

INTPs respond well to challenges and are adept at improving situations or finding new pieces to complete a puzzle. They hunger for problems to solve.

INTPs are devoted to accuracy and are inclined to sometimes split hairs. They observe differences in groups of data and are able to pinpoint inconsistencies that most people overlook.

INTPs need to be continually stimulated and find it difficult to work on mundane or routine projects. They are not administrative people, but intellectuals who apply their energy to researching or analysing issues.

INTPs do not concern themselves with practicalities. Concepts, ideas and working on hypotheses are motivating to them. They enjoy establishing theories and then proving or disproving them.

Relationships INTPs are often perceived to be aloof. They enjoy their own company in order to think and contemplate. They have difficulty expressing feelings and do not generally show appreciation. In addition, INTPs often appear to be critical (which they are) through their demeanour or body language even though nothing much has been said.

Essentially, INTPs are loners. They need relationships for the practical benefits of companionship and sharing, but they also need to be understood (especially by extroverts) and be given time for themselves.

INTPs are not likely to have a wide range of friends. Instead, they have a few deep friendships with people who share their interests and conceptual orientation.

Counter-productive tendencies It is important for INTPs to find acceptance and be appreciated for their intellect. If not, they become frustrated and withdraw into themselves, adopting a negative and cynical attitude; they can, at times, become sarcastic and critical to the point that it is destructive.

INTPs are so analytical and logical that they fail to appreciate how others value sentiment. Consequently, they often overlook the value of an apology, a compliment, a smile, a thank you and spending time listening to the concerns of others. It's not that they are unkind; they simply do not think in terms of feelings.

INTPs can also be somewhat impractical and forgetful of everyday details such as paying accounts and attending to their physical needs.

ESFJ

In a nutshell ESFJs are outgoing, practical and organised people. They enjoy interacting with others and are warm and friendly. They are also conscientious and can be relied upon to complete tasks accurately and on time.

Words that characterise the ESFJ psychological type are:

- responsible;
- harmonious;
- thorough;
- compassionate;
- practical;
- responsive; and
- traditional.

General characteristics ESFJs are gregarious and outgoing. Personal interaction is important to them and they are skilled at making people feel comfortable. Friendly, cooperative and tactful, ESFJs make a consistent effort to say and do the right thing. They are encouraged by appreciation and approval, and hurt by indifference or tactlessness.

Conflict-ridden situations make ESFJs uncomfortable and they try, as far as possible, to ensure that these do not occur.

ESFJs expect a great deal from themselves and, when they fall short of their expectations, they come down hard on themselves.

ESFJs focus on the here-and-now and base their decisions on known facts and past experience. They do not like taking risks and will protect themselves against exposures as far as possible.

ESFJs are particular with detail and cope well with routine. They are practical people who need to see the results of their efforts.

ESFJs are put off by theory. To them theories are abstract ideas that have little relevance until they can be put to use.

ESFJs are decisive and thorough in what they do. They plan well and complete projects on time even if it means extending themselves beyond the call of duty. They are not entirely happy until decisions are made and jobs completed, and they push themselves to this end.

ESFJs are also sensitive to the needs of others. They care about people and much of their satisfaction comes from the relationships they experience. They value family and social ties.

ESFJs like to preserve traditions. To them, traditional values and behaviours provide stability and consistency. Rituals, ceremonies and celebrations give ESFJs a sense of belonging and permanence.

ESFJs are hard workers who are not afraid of taking responsibility. They can be counted on to finish whatever they start.

ESFJs value ownership. They seek to acquire, possess and preserve items, including property. This fulfils their need for roots, something tangible to hold on to, which is evident in their appreciation of home.

ESFJs are definite and specific in the way they talk. They don't like metaphors or abstractions. Their thought processes are step-by-step and linear. They like to handle one thing at a time; addressing too many important things simultaneously may be a source of stress.

Relationships   Belonging is very important to ESFJs. They emphasise social ties and enjoy socialising with many friends. ESFJs see their workplace as a place to serve and help others.

Because ESFJs are caring people, they are involved in their relationships, readily giving and receiving. However, their gifts will be practical and their displays of emotion moderate rather than effusive.

ESFJs are loyal and, when relationships end, are inclined to perceive it as a personal failure.

Counter-productive tendencies

ESFJs' strong desire to please and achieve results may cause them to ignore their own needs. In the extreme this leads to burnout. Consequently, they need to learn to say "no" and look after themselves without feeling that they will disappoint others.

ESFJs are resistant to change. They like to stay with the known, and feel insecure with the unknown, or any skill they have not mastered.

Because ESFJs have a need to finish projects and reach conclusions, they may decide too quickly, with inadequate data. Furthermore, they are inclined to overlook the long-term consequences of current decisions and may fail to see the wider ramifications.

When stressed, ESFJs become uncharacteristically critical of others and of themselves. In these circumstances the immediate need to get things done overrides their normal sensitivities. This behaviour often troubles them later, at which time they are inclined to feel remorseful.

ENFJ

In a nutshell ENFJs are charismatic, sociable and well-organised people. They honour their commitments and expect others to do the same.

ENFJs enjoy developing people, encouraging them to use their potential and accomplish as much as possible. They are also good communicators.

Words that describe the ENFJ psychological type are:

- supportive;
- tenacious;
- outgoing;
- persuasive;
- responsible;
- affable; and
- organised.

General characteristics The chief concern of ENFJs is to enable people to develop their capabilities. They are driven by warm personal interactions, fostering harmony and communications. Thus ENFJs are friendly, cooperative and tactful. They take care to say and do the right thing.

ENFJs are well-organised people. They do not like disorganisation and will prepare schedules and plans, together with objectives so that they have a clear idea of what needs to be achieved. Then they get into action and "just do it".

ENFJs are patient and conscientious. They make a concerted effort to stick with a job until it is completed.

ENFJs have very clear values, beliefs and, given the authority, they will insist that others adhere to what they consider to be right.

ENFJs seek to find meaning in who they are and what they do. They tend to be humanitarian and are motivated by contributing to the welfare of others.

ENFJs are curious and imaginative. They enjoy exploring possibilities and see connections that less intuitive types are likely to miss.

ENFJs like communicating. They are good speakers and facilitators, skilfully blending a concern for people with the need to achieve results. Consequently, they are perceived as persuasive and influential.

ENFJs are loyal. However, their loyalty is more towards people and causes than to organisations. They are committed to the progress and growth of those around them and this takes precedence over procedures and rules.

ENFJs like variety and fun. Yet they are also

dedicated to achieving results, both individually and as members of a team. These attributes, though, may cause them to overcommit themselves and become somewhat frayed by taking on too many tasks, and being pulled in several directions at once.

ENFJs are enthusiastic people. They believe in themselves and in their undertakings and they see good in everyone and everything. While this is an admirable trait, they may overlook the 'dark side' and become disappointed when reality fails to measure up to their expectations.

ENFJs usually have a good sense of humour. They are often the 'life and soul of the party'.

Relationships ENFJs are romantic people. For them, expressions of love involve flowers, surprises, candlelit dinners with sentimental music in the background, and the like.

ENFJs commit themselves to establishing harmonious and fruitful relationships with others. When commitments are broken, they take it personally. When relationships go through rough patches, ENFJs are particularly hard hit; they do not easily cope with disharmony.

Counter-productive tendencies

ENFJs seek to please others so much that they take criticism personally. Negative feedback, of whatever kind, hurts and, rather than face the issue, they are inclined towards avoidant behaviour.

ENFJs tend to base their decisions on how they feel. If they do not support this tendency with a rational evaluation of facts, their decisions may, at times, be inconsistent and illogical.

If ENFJs do not find a place where their talents can be put to good use they become frustrated and start to doubt themselves, engaging in self-criticism and self-downing.

Under stress, ENFJs act in uncharacteristic ways. They are likely to withdraw into themselves and become highly critical – sometimes verbalising these opinions, other times not. This can be confusing to others and upsetting for the ENFJ, who will probably feel guilty afterwards.

ISFP

In a nutshell ISFPs are quiet, reserved people who are somewhat shy and retiring. They are quite happy to work on their own and will usually be found doing things of a practical nature.

ISFPs are caring people who are sensitive to the needs of others. They are also free spirits who value their independence.

Words that describe this psychological type are:

- adaptable;
- caring;
- observant;
- spontaneous;
- reserved;
- sensitive; and
- pleasure-seeking.

General characteristics ISFPs are quiet, pragmatic people. They get on with things without much fuss and do whatever needs to be done with a minimum of effort.

ISFPs are at their best when responding to crises. They work particularly well with people in need, and are able to adapt to whatever situation confronts them.

ISFPs need to be challenged, otherwise their energies are likely to be diffused into pleasure-seeking activities rather than goal-oriented ones. At the same time they require variety. Dealing with many issues simultaneously is something that ISFPs do easily.

ISFPs are compassionate people who are open and flexible. They are considerate and will neither negate the views of others, nor seek to dominate others. Instead, they attend to the needs of people in a quiet, modest manner. The well-being of others is important to them.

ISFPs learn best through their senses. They need to experience things and work with them to fully understand. Thus, they are not drawn to theories and concepts, and prefer practical subjects.

ISFPs do not like to be forced into a mould. They are spontaneous people who value the freedom to experience a wide variety of activities.

Always seeking opportunities, ISFPs are willing to change their positions when new facts are brought to their attention. Yet at the same time they do not like to stray too far from the familiar and may be uncomfortable with changes that are imposed upon them.

ISFPs are optimistic and cheerful. They dislike predictions of doom and gloom, and look for the best in situations.

ISFPs are skilled at applying practical methods to overcome obstacles. They are averse to policies and procedures, and frequently ignore directives, relying on their better judgement.

ISFPs are inclined to act on their feelings. Doing things out of duty, responsibility, or because it is expected, does not appeal to them.

ISFPs engage themselves in present realities. Future events are somewhere out there that may or may not happen; what is happening now is what matters most.

Relationships Relationships are important to ISFPs because they value harmonious interactions. Consideration for the needs of others is a cornerstone quality and they will go to great lengths to be of service.

Because loving and being loved is crucial to ISFPs they will do whatever it takes to ensure that relationships are nurtured and continue to grow.

ISFPs may find it difficult to express the richness of their inner worlds. They are concrete and specific in their use of words and generally find conversation inadequate to reveal their feelings. For them actions speak louder than words.

Counter-productive tendencies Because ISFPs are tactical rather than strategic thinkers, they tend to go for quick-fixes and become irritated with longer-term or more permanent solutions. Thus they are inclined to be short-sighted, not looking beyond the present to place things in a wider context.

ISFPs are very giving of themselves and are easily hurt when others do not respond favourably. In such circumstances they tend to withdraw into themselves.

When stressed, ISFPs can become unusually critical of themselves and others.

INFP

In a nutshell INFPs have a definite set of values that guide their behaviours and influence their decisions. They seek work that is meaningful to them and which contributes to their growth and development.

INFPs are restrained people who are not particularly demonstrative. Yet they display an unusual commitment to both the people and the causes they support.

Words that describe this psychological type are:

- value-driven;
- committed;
- contemplative;
- empathetic;
- loyal;
- sensitive; and
- creative.

General characteristics INFPs are quiet, sensitive people who are often perceived by others to be shy. They are idealistic, with a strong sense of purpose. For them work is a calling and they abhor organisational politics and profiteering at the expense of others. They also dislike it when people are abused or manipulated.

INFPs do not like competition. They believe that each

individual should be encouraged to do his or her best and people should not be pitted against one another. Cooperation and teamwork are important to them.

INFPs are motivated by principles and values that are specific. They make it a priority to live according to these values and it is this that gives validity and meaning to their behaviours.

INFPs enjoy taking in information and reflecting on it. They are creative individuals who see connections and possibilities for change. Thus they are constantly growing and trying out new things.

INFPs find new experiences fascinating. However, they tend to work with bursts of energy. When inspired they put in a great deal of effort and become fully engaged. Then, when the novelty wears off, or when challenges have been met, they find it difficult to motivate themselves. Ideally, therefore, INFPs work best when they are able to initiate a project and hand it over as soon as it gets to the maintenance stage.

INFPs are often perfectionists. They are idealists who, because of a strong sense of calling, have a need to achieve. However, they tend to have unrealistic expectations of themselves and others, and are inclined to be discouraged when a gap exists between their ideals and the results accomplished.

Relationships   INFPs have a strong need for meaningful relationships based on genuine caring. They are not frivolous people. Authenticity is of great importance and INFPs abhor superficial or manipulative liaisons.

INFPs expect relationships to grow and develop. They know that nothing is constant and, for them, support and understanding are long-term, self-imposed disciplines.

INFPs are disturbed by conflict. Instead of facing things, they tend to ignore conflict for as long as possible. However, when pushed, INFPs are able to marshal their inner resources and address matters; they usually resolve whatever problems they face.

Counter-productive tendencies   INFPs become so absorbed in projects that interest them that they have a tendency to neglect their own needs. As a consequence, they could burn themselves out or, alternatively, come to resent themselves. It is important, therefore, for INFPs to allocate personal time for relaxation and renewal.

Because INFPs are usually responsive to the needs of others they are inclined to blame themselves for the failures of other people even though such blame is irrational.

INFPs are visionaries. Sometimes, however, they have unrealistic expectations. This leads to feelings of incompetence and worthlessness when things do not work out.

ESTP

In a nutshell ESTPs are good communicators who have an ability to influence others and settle disputes; they encourage agreement and suggest solutions, yet rarely impose their opinions on others. ESTPs are, therefore, good mediators. In addition, they are action-oriented, practical and realistic people who thrive on doing things efficiently.

Words that describe this psychological type are:

- spontaneous;
- rational;
- influential;
- practical;
- easy-going; and
- resourceful.

General characteristics ESTPs are influential people. Adept at interpreting what people need, they anticipate the behaviours of others and respond accordingly. These attributes cause people to have confidence in them. ESTPs are, therefore, natural negotiators, diplomats, entrepreneurs and salespeople.

ESTPs live in the fast lane. They seek to make the most of life. They thrive on action and are lively and entertaining.

ESTPs live in the present moment. Others may see them as goal-oriented but, in reality, most ESTPs are motivated by their immediate passions and interests. They find work and play inseparable, deriving pleasure from doing things that reflect their interests. Thus they are more action-oriented than goal-oriented.

This does not mean that ESTPs cannot stick to tasks. They can, but it takes an effort not to move on to other pursuits after the excitement has worn off. These people, after all, are adventurous types.

ESTPs are good at dealing with crisis situations. Crises are opportunities for them to marshal their resources and show their capabilities.

ESTPs are practical people. They are down-to-earth and impatient with theories or abstractions. Their orientation is to solve problems that are specific and concrete, and provide a short-term payoff.

In leadership roles, ESTPs are regarded as logical trouble-shooters since they thrive on solving problems. They have a keen sense of reality and a talent for spotting trouble early. Their capacity for focusing on the here-and-now often leads to beneficial short-term results.

Always on the lookout to exploit opportunities, ESTPs are adaptable. They are prepared to amend their positions if new facts are presented or the scenario changes. However, they do not like change for its own sake and are likely to be uncomfortable with transformations that they themselves have not introduced or been consulted on.

ESTPs dislike repetition, rules and bureaucracy. When confronted with these, they quickly find ways to vary routines.

Relationships ESTPs are easy to get along with. They are exciting and inspiring people who network well and have a wide variety of friends. People are drawn to ESTPs because of their charm and charisma, as well as their preference for action and fun. When rejected, ESTPs feel hurt for a while, then decide that it's useless to indulge in negative emotions, and they move on.

Counter-productive tendencies ESTPs need a great deal of stimulation and variety. They quickly take on new projects and get things going with great gusto. However, they are not so keen to see assignments through to completion, especially if projects are long-term or if they become boring; there are too many exciting things that clamour for their attention.

ESTPs are so engaged in current realities that they seldom look ahead. Consequently, they tend to look for quick fixes and may overlook the long-term implications of their decisions and actions.

ESTPs can be very demanding. Not being contemplative types, they seldom spend a great deal of time thinking. Their unspoken motto is act first, think later. They also need to be reminded to listen to others and consider what others have to say, and how others feel, before jumping in.

ESFP

In a nutshell ESFPs are friendly, optimistic people who seek to enjoy life. They like to be where the action is, and are gifted in observing human behaviour and establishing what people want. They are empathetic. They are also generous with their time and possessions.

Words that describe the ESFP psychological type are:

- enthusiastic;
- sociable;
- fun-loving;
- optimistic;
- open-minded;
- adaptable; and
- cooperative.

General characteristics ESFPs are warm, outgoing individuals who believe that life, work and relationships should be meaningful and fun. They are exuberant, with a wide variety of friends and are generally well liked.

ESFPs are at their best in company; they dislike isolation and being alone for long periods.

ESFPs are action-oriented. Passivity and contemplation do not go well with them. They are not enamoured of concepts or abstractions based on philosophical ideas. If whatever is required of them does not need some sort of action, they get bored and lose interest.

ESFPs are optimistic people. They expect things to go well and are prepared to take risks that are avoided by more conservative types.

ESFPs have a zest for living. They revel in the comforts and attractions of life - good food, quality entertainment, travel, nice car, fine home and so on. They are, therefore, inclined to direct their time, energy and skills to acquiring material possessions and having a good time.

ESFPs have an eye for spotting new opportunities. They are adaptable and quickly change their views or positions when new information is presented to them. They are also pragmatic people who, when faced with implementing solutions, will ask, "Will it work?" and "Is it practical?"

ESFPs, though seeking adventure and variety, do not like change imposed on them. They want to control their destinies and tend to resist changes they have not introduced themselves.

With their attention focused on the present moment, and their practical natures, ESFPs are able to solve problems effectively – especially people problems. By nature they are free spirits and, therefore, do not feel the need to rigidly apply rules and regulations. Consequently, they are likely to find ways of solving problems by adapting and bending rules rather than being led by them.

ESFPs usually base their decisions on factors that are important to them instead of on logical analyses of impersonal facts. Since they are empathetic by nature, they usually take human needs into account when they make decisions.

SFPs learn best by becoming involved through hands-on activities. Listening to lectures and spending time with books is not how they like to learn. Also, learning is not undertaken for its own sake but for how it can be used, and the result it is likely to produce.

Relationships ESFPs need people. They find their meaning in work that involves people; human contact is essential for their well-being. They, therefore, have a wide range of friendships and spend a great deal of time cultivating relationships.

ESFPs also need to be in an intimate relationship with someone. They are afraid of rejection and of being alone.

Counter-productive tendencies ESFPs tend to procrastinate on jobs that do not excite them. They generally leave things to the last moment, and rush to complete projects on time.

Planning and managing time are usually weak areas

for ESFPs. They are frequently so involved in activities that interest them that they lose track of time and fail to give attention to other matters that are important. However, it needs to be said that ESFPs are masters of 'winging it' and coping in unprepared situations.

ESFPs have a short-term perspective. They seldom develop strategies for the future or take stock of where they are going. This makes them vulnerable.

With their hunger for spontaneity and variety, ESFPs may be considered somewhat irresponsible and unpredictable by those who would like them to be more organised.

ISTJ

In a nutshell ISTJs are serious, reserved people. They are meticulous individuals who can be relied upon to see things through. Practical and methodical, ISTJs take responsibility for their work.

Words that describe this psychological type are:

- factual;
- dependable;
- sensible;
- organised;
- practical;
- duty-bound; and
- thorough.

General characteristics ISTJs are practical and realistic people who are hard-working, responsible and thorough in all they do. They can be counted on to never undertake a project or relationship impulsively or frivolously. Consequently, ISTJs are very concerned about making sure things are right; it is important that they remain in control of situations because quality and good work are points of honour for them.

ISTJs like to have things clearly stated. Thus they become frustrated when situations are ambiguous or uncertain.

As a general rule, ISTJs need to feel that they are

useful and are making a difference. Their sense of obligation is a driving force, pushing them to take on a great number of tasks, sometimes to their own detriment.

Other people are likely to admire ISTJs for their dogged application, sense of duty and accomplishments. Yet ISTJs typically do not believe in themselves. They usually underestimate their talents and abilities, often focusing on their flaws.

ISTJs take an objective, logical approach to decision-making. They need to get facts and are systematic in gathering and interpreting data. They are thus practical, sensible and realistic.

ISTJs also have definite views about the subjects that interest them. This is because they have arrived at conclusions by applying logical criteria based on thought and sound reasoning.

ISTJs' thought processes are linear and step-by-step. Consequently, they are not likely to be particularly creative. In fact, they frown on new ideas if they contradict tried-and-tested methods.

ISTJs like to handle one thing at a time. Situations where things happen simultaneously, at many levels, are stressful to them.

Relationships For an ISTJ a relationship means commitment. They dislike associations purely for the purpose of convenience. This also applies to being a member of a team. ISTJs want to know that members are supportive of one another and are dedicated to ensuring the well-being of the group and the achievement of objectives.

ISTJs are not demonstrative. They are unlikely to freely give compliments and, if they do, it will not usually be in public. Similarly, ISTJs do not feel comfortable receiving open praise or, indeed, expressions of feelings in public.

ISTJs also need space for themselves. While they may enjoy interacting with others, they find such activities draining and need time alone to recharge their batteries, so to speak.

Counter-productive tendencies ISTJs have a tendency to overuse their strengths. This is because they tend to perceive things as right or wrong, with little flexibility in adapting to different situations. They may also become detail bound, overwhelming others with technicalities, and ignoring the bigger issues.

If ISTJs feel unappreciated for their work, duty and loyalty, they become frustrated because they link their worth to their values and what they do. Thus their self-esteem suffers, resulting in defensive behaviour such as:

- setting rigid rules and procedures and doing things "by the book", and

- being critical and judgemental of themselves and others.

Under stress, ISTJs typically see the worst in situations. They indulge in imagining negative and even catastrophic results, for themselves and others.

ISTJs are also so focused on what needs to be done that they tend to ignore the human element – the feelings that people have. In addition, they are inclined to overlook pleasantries and expressions of appreciation.

ISFJ

In a nutshell   ISFJs are sensitive, compassionate people who are considerate and conscientious. They are very loyal and will go to almost any trouble to help people whom they care about.

ISFJs are practical people who have a need to find meaning in their work. They are often self-effacing and don't mind working quietly in the background.

Words that describe this psychological type are:

* traditional;
* reserved;
* well-organised;
* responsible;
* practical;
* meticulous; and
* loyal.

General characteristics   ISFJs may be described as reserved people who are relatively easy going, yet have a strong sense of duty to their calling, whatever that may be. They find their energy within and need space to recharge themselves and think through matters.

ISFJs find their reality in practical, concrete issues - things that can be seen, touched or experienced. Theories or conceptual ideas have little validity unless they can be used in ways that make a difference, particularly to the lives of others.

ISFJs are extremely dependable. They can be counted on to be there when needed and will diligently apply themselves to tasks at hand. They are usually well organised, structured people who might complain and moan from time to time, but who will, nevertheless, take on and carry out what needs to be done.

Because duty, responsibility and adhering to rules permeate all that ISFJs do, their lifestyles are characterised by caring for, and serving, others. They focus on what people need and want, and they establish orderly procedures for making things happen.

Being independent is important to ISFJs. Yet, paradoxically, they are unlikely to become free spirits, unfettered by the demands of others. The reason is that they have a strong need to feel useful and needed; they are almost driven by obligation. Consequently, ISFJs often experience internal conflict - the dissonance between what they would like and the call of duty.

ISFJs value possessions. They find security in owning objects, including property. They take care of things and expect others to do the same. Waste and unnecessary consumption unsettle them.

ISFJs are also conservative with their finances. They protect their future by looking after money matters.

ISFJs will not gamble away their hard-earned rewards, nor are they likely to take unreasonable risks. They believe in saving money to provide for possible misfortunes.

Relationships ISFJs have a deep need to direct their energies towards service to others. Relationships are, therefore, all-important.

ISFJs are unassuming and quiet in their interactions, often putting the needs of others, especially family members, ahead of their own. They, therefore, make excellent team players and function best when all are focused on an overarching purpose or mission.

ISFJs are not competitive. They are disturbed by adversarial relationships, and seeking to win over others. Achieving results as a group is far more important than standing out as an individual. ISFJs are, therefore, cooperative, harmonious people.

In their personal lives, ISFJs tend to gravitate towards people who have problems or noticeable weaknesses. Their caring nature draws them towards those to whom they can minister. ISFJs are, therefore, vulnerable to being caught up in co-dependent relationships where their partners depend on them for strength and support, and they derive unconscious satisfaction (though it may not be a particularly happy one) from feeling needed.

Counter-productive tendencies

ISFJs desire to serve others, and their loyalty, may cause them to neglect their own needs. Add to this the inner conflict of seeking to be independent, yet needing others, and you have the ingredients for potential burnout unless they make a concerted effort to make time for themselves.

When stressed, ISFJs tend to focus so much on what should be, or should not be, that they can behave in quite uncharacteristic ways, losing sight of what people really need. They can also be quite stubborn in such circumstances.

ISFJs like order and stability. It is not surprising, therefore, that they do not like change, especially change that is imposed on them or that threatens their secure and known activities.

ISFJs value harmony so much that they are inclined to avoid confrontation. When people let them down they become resentful, often without speaking out or letting the offender know of his/her deeds. Also, ISFJs may, at times, find it difficult to communicate with others in adverse circumstances. Being polite and considerate may overrule their normal desire to take action.

ENTP

In a nutshell

ENTPs are innovative people who enjoy the challenges of change. They see possibilities in situations and are enterprising and resourceful in overcoming problems to achieve their goals.

ENTPs dislike routine. They are inclined, therefore, to enthusiastically embrace new projects that excite them, but quickly become bored with challenges that have been met or when a more exciting assignment grabs their attention.

Words that describe this psychological type are:
- analytical;
- innovative;
- curious;
- adaptive;
- independent thinker;
- resourceful; and
- energetic.

General characteristics

ENTPs tend to live in the future. They are highly energetic people who tirelessly pursue new assignments and come up with creative ideas.

ENTPs are independent thinkers. They do not rely on others to form an opinion and are very adept at seeking flaws. Being 'big-picture' people, they quickly notice how parts fit into the overall scheme of things. They are good at generating conceptual possibilities, and developing innovative strategies to achieve their goals.

ENTPs enjoy learning. They are fascinated by concepts and theories and continuously strive for self-improvement. They learn through interactive discussions, by challenging the status quo and by questioning the validity of existing positions. Furthermore, they thrive on intellectual tasks through which they can demonstrate their thinking skills and creativity.

ENTPs like to take risks and explore new possibilities. They constantly scan their environment for ideas or activities that are new and different.

Travel is important to most ENTPs because it permits new experiences and opens the way for new understandings of diverse cultures. Many ENTPs also involve themselves in unusual physical activities, such as sky-diving or mountain climbing, in which they stretch themselves physically and find the excitement that comes from doing something different.

ENTPs usually enjoy reading, not because it isolates them from others but because it lets their active minds reflect, link ideas and fantasise.

ENTPs have a high need for achievement. However, such achievement is not necessarily measured by what society values or by the norms of other people. Remember that ENTPs are very independent and, therefore, need to excel in whatever is meaningful to them. This need for achievement is increased by an ever-present, though concealed, fear of failure.

Relationships

ENTPs need relationships that are stimulating and exciting. On the one hand they meet people easily, are comfortable with them and quickly make friends. However, they tend to spread their friendships broadly and move from one person to another; they are inclined to tire of people as easily as they tire of projects that do not inspire them.

Counter-productive tendencies

ENTPs are inclined to overlook feelings in their search for objective understanding. This is particularly true when illogical ideas are presented or when irrational emotions come to the fore. In such circumstances ENTPs can be intolerant and bitingly critical of what they perceive as thoughts and behaviours that make no sense.

ENTPs are conceptual thinkers who like to dwell on possibilities rather than practicalities. They are likely to generate stimulating ideas and are moved to action with only a rough plan or broad strategy in mind. This trait can be very valuable in initiating change, but it can also create problems in that ENTPs usually neglect to attend to detail and carry out the necessary preparations that would ensure the success of a project. It often happens that, in their haste to accomplish what they perceive as exciting goals, they overlook what they regard as minor issues only to find that these turn up later as major hurdles.

Another weakness of ENTPs is that they get things going with great gusto, but lose interest as soon as challenges are met or a more exciting project comes up; they tend to be great starters but poor finishers. To overcome this, they need to be more selective in what they commit themselves to and make a concerted effort to stay with their chosen projects until completed.

ENTPs are inclined to place great value on material possessions. They can get so wrapped up in acquiring status symbols that they forget that real meaning and fulfilment are not found in objects.

ENFP

In a nutshell ENFPs are people who initiate change. They love variety and see new possibilities in all manner of things.

ENFPs are highly energetic people who have many interests. They bring enthusiasm, joy and fun into all aspects of their lives. New projects stimulate them and they are at their best in situations that are fluid and changing, allowing them to innovate and influence.

ENFPs are sensitive people who anticipate the needs of others and readily offer help and encouragement.

Words that describe the ENFP psychological type are:

- spontaneous;
- imaginative;
- friendly;
- energetic;
- enthusiastic;
- perceptive; and
- adventurous.

General characteristics For ENFPs life is a creative adventure, full of exciting possibilities. They are perceptive people who are very aware of what is going on around them.

ENFPs joyfully immerse themselves in life's activities

and are very quick to start projects. However, because they dislike mundane and routine activities, they are likely to abandon projects when they become boring; in other words they tend to neglect seeing projects through to completion.

ENFPs are the dreamers of this world. They are intensely curious and use their imagination to adapt, change and re-invent the world around them. ENFPs are stimulated by change, ideas and new experiences. They see connections in situations, and find significance and meaning in varied activities.

ENFPs prefer working with imaginative, action-oriented people. They seek an attractive, colourful environment that reflects their creative and enthusiastic natures. The perfect job would offer novelty, challenge, diversity and a relative freedom from burdensome policies and procedures.

ENFPs often have a difficult time separating their work and private lives. Because they incorporate fun in their work, the boundaries between work and play are not clearly delineated.

Integrity is very important to ENFPs. They have a very clear and definite code of what constitutes right and wrong, and often strive for the 'greater good' of all. ENFPs generally see the good and positive in people and situations. From this idealistic perspective they are inclined to be disappointed when reality does not measure up. Nevertheless, they do not remain down for long, always looking ahead and not wasting too much time on the upsets of the past.

ENFPs are quite happy living in a diverse and changing world. They find ambiguity and paradox easy to deal with; they enjoy seeing things from different perspectives. Thus orderly, systematic and predictable behaviours and systems are turn-offs for ENFPs.

Relationships ENFPs are enthusiastic and gregarious people with many friends. They have a wide range of interests and value genuineness in their relationships. Because people are important to ENFPs, they go to great lengths to develop and nurture relationships through open communication, loyalty and support.

ENFPs are sensitive individuals who are quick to express appreciation. They seem to know just what to say and do to make other people feel wanted. In fact, ENFPs are naturals in encouraging and inspiring others.

Counter-productive tendencies A constant issue with most ENFPs is that they become so caught up in a stream of new, exciting ideas, tasks and projects that they move in many directions at once. This lack of focus, with an inability to turn off their minds, inclines them to overload themselves by taking on too many tasks at the same time. Also, because they abhor routine, they become bored when the initial excitement of a new project has worn off and they, therefore, fail to follow through. Consequently, ENFPs are likely to be perceived as scatty people who are great starters but poor finishers.

ENFPs are highly creative, big-picture thinkers. As valuable as these attributes are, they pose a problem when they are overused. In other words ENFPs are inclined to overlook details and practical matters while becoming obsessed with possibilities.

Because ENFPs are full of zest and fun loving, they may neglect everyday responsibilities, squandering their energies on exciting yet ill-chosen tasks. This characteristic is frequently resented by those who have to pick up after them or complete what has been left undone.

Under great stress ENFPs behave in uncharacteristic ways; they become overwhelmed by detail, lose their normal perspective and possessiveness, and let their problems and concerns consume their everyday thoughts.

INTJ

In a nutshell

INTJs are self-confident, individualistic thinkers. They have a clear vision of the future and are creative in finding solutions to problems and seeing new possibilities in everyday situations.

Words that describe this psychological type are:

- independent;
- critical;
- visionary;
- logical;
- reserved;
- organised; and
- demanding.

General characteristics

INTJs are tenacious individualists who want to control as much of their worlds as possible. They are very determined people who know what they want and who trust their own judgements, regardless of what others may think.

INTJs are thinkers. Reserved by nature, they contemplate all manner of situations from a global perspective, making connections and quickly relating new information to overall patterns. It is not surprising, therefore, that INTJs are good at strategy. They take a bird's eye view and can integrate information while observing patterns. Thus they are generally insightful visionaries who have a clear picture of future trends and possibilities.

INTJs make rational and logical decisions. They evaluate data critically and are quick to spot inconsistent information or irrelevant data. It is difficult to 'pull the wool over the eyes' of INTJs.

INTJs are organised people. They abhor inefficiency and confusion and usually plan their work so that things get done on time.

INTJs are good problem solvers. They combine sound logic with the exploration of creative possibilities and often come up with innovative solutions. It is not surprising, therefore, that INTJs enjoy challenges that provide opportunities for them to demonstrate their capabilities.

INTJs are achievement-oriented people who are single-minded about their work. They have a sense of urgency and will not let go of a task or project until it has been satisfactorily completed. INTJs are thus somewhat impatient with, and intolerant of, people whom they perceive as inefficient.

INTJs direct their energies towards acquiring knowledge, competence and the furthering of their visions of future possibilities.

INTJs work best with decisive, thinking people who have clear goals. They prefer a task-oriented workplace with space for privacy and time to reflect. Problem-solving opportunities and challenges are also important. INTJs operate independently and have little need to be part of a team – unless teams provide a platform for generating ideas and establishing a future direction.

Relationships   INTJs tend to be reserved individualists who prefer to do things on their own rather than subject themselves to being part of a group. At one level, therefore, it appears that they have little need of others. Certainly INTJs do not need others for approval, nor do they need people for affirmation. However, they do require others to share their visions and enable them to achieve their goals.

In their private lives, INTJs have a very specific idea of what a relationship ought to be. This perception is likely to be somewhat idealistic with roles clearly defined.

INTJs are introverted people who do not easily share their feelings and affections. However, they are very loyal and caring and will go to any lengths to protect those whom they love.

When rejected, INTJs retreat into their own world, sharing few (if any) of their feelings. They act as though nothing has happened although, if provoked, will lash out with criticism of others. On the surface it appears that INTJs cope very well with matters of the heart that go wrong but, in reality, they take a long time to recover.

Counter-productive tendencies

INTJs tend to ignore the impact of their temperament on others. This is exacerbated by the fact that they care little for what others think. Consequently people regard them as emotionally detached, critical and opinionated.

INTJs are somewhat idealistic. Being 'big-picture' people they can be impractical, often not considering whether their concepts are workable. They are also often perceived as intellectual snobs with little patience for those who cannot understand their ideas. While they do not like to be perceived as arrogant, this is often how others see them.

INFJ

In a nutshell INFJs are reserved people who are compassionate and seek to live in harmony with others. They have a clearly defined set of values that provide meaning and guidelines for daily living. INFJs are at their best when working on issues that further the welfare and development of people.

Words that describe this psychological type are:

- committed;
- sensitive;
- loyal;
- creative;
- reserved;
- caring; and
- idealistic.

General characteristics INFJs are intuitive individuals who see things from an overall perspective and are able to connect new information to larger patterns. They are constantly searching for meanings in words, in people and in situations. For INFJs there is a reason and purpose behind everything, and understanding the dynamics behind behaviours and events is more important than the substance of the specific events.

INFJs are reserved, introverted people who have deep, intense feelings. However, they have difficulty sharing what they feel, not because they are afraid to do so but because, in the moment, they cannot always find the precise words to express the depth of their emotions. Consequently, many INFJs find that writing is a more appropriate medium for communicating their thoughts and feelings. This gives them time to formulate their ideas and present them using verbal images and metaphors. They usually write well and often express themselves in unique and artistic ways.

INFJs seek meaning and purpose in all aspects of their lives as they are value driven. Personal development and growth, in themselves and others, are important to them.

INFJs are skilled at anything to do with people. They are good listeners and are empathetic. However, rather than involve themselves superficially with many people, they prefer one-on-one relationships. Intimacy is more important than quantity. Therefore, one should not expect INFJs to be comfortable in crowds or large groups. Typically, they dislike being the centre of attention or addressing large groups of people.

Seeing connections is a skill that most INFJs have. They are also contemplative people who have a capacity for deep concentration. These two qualities give INFJs knowledge and insights that are beyond the discernment of most people.

INFJs seek predictability and order in their lives. They

dislike confusion and like to work on one project at a time, completing whatever they set out to do. Starting many projects simultaneously, or having many loose ends, does not fit with their idea of effectiveness.

Relationships INFJs' first commitment is to people. They value human relationships so strongly that they become concerned and involved with the problems of their loved ones, friends and co-workers.

INFJs are very adept at expressing appreciation and finding suitable opportunities to encourage people. They give recognition and provide a warm, supportive environment to further the development of meaningful, harmonious relations.

Counter-productive tendencies INFJs are inclined to focus so much on the human element that they tend to overlook everyday tasks. They are also prone to lose sight of their own needs (while serving everyone else's needs) and suffer a loss of personal identity, eventually burning out if corrective measures are not taken.

While INFJs are adaptable people, they find processes and procedures frustrating, especially if they are applied in a bureaucratic manner. Consequently, in an attempt to create a working environment that gives people freedom and autonomy (and one that encourages individual growth) they may not apply rules. This could create conflict because, on the one hand, INFJs like to be well organised but, on the other hand, they have difficulty working within defined constraints.

INFJs tend to be idealistic and perfectionistic. They, therefore, are inclined to put off tasks rather than accept imperfect products and conditions. In addition, they also sometimes live in the world of fantasy, preferring dreams to reality.

Under great stress INFJs become obsessive. They engage in repetitive activities, overindulge in habits that provide comfort (such as eating) and tend to spend excessively, perhaps even buying things they do not need.

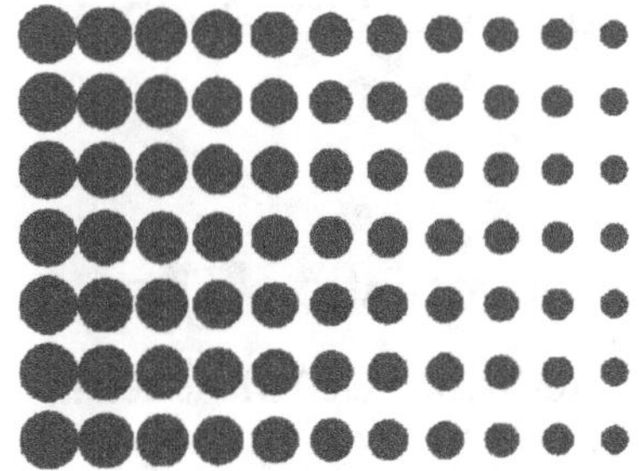

4

Frequently asked
questions about
Psychological Type

Frequently asked questions about Psychological Type

Where do preferences come from? Most people want to know whether we inherit our temperaments, or develop them through experiences and social interactions. In other words, what determines our temperaments - nature or nurture?

In my view, both genetics and environment play significant roles in the development of traits. How much of one or the other, nobody knows.

There is ample evidence to support both positions. For example, psychologists are able to show that identical twins, who are genetically similar, have common habits and characteristics even though they were separated at an early age and brought up in very different environments.

On the other hand, genetics cannot explain how one person can demonstrate totally different personalities from the disorder technically known as "Dissociated Identity Disorder", i.e. someone with multiple personalities. Also, experience can cause a radical shift in personality, for example, an outgoing child may suddenly become withdrawn and introverted as a result of a traumatic encounter.

There is no doubt that we are born with certain predispositions or preferences. These are, however, shaped, developed, restricted and even suppressed by the environment in which we live.

Our behaviours, therefore, reflect both genetic factors and the influences of our environment. Nature and nurture are, together, responsible for our preferences.

Are some "types" better than others?

There are definitely no "better" types.

Identifying Psychological Type simply reveals dominant preferences. And preferences, on their own, indicate only pre-existing inclinations.

Is it, therefore, better to have a natural inclination towards being organised rather than flexible (i.e. the J vs. P dimensions)? The truth is that each is disposed to tackle issues and deal with events in a different way and neither is superior to the other.

Consider, for example, the true case of two public speakers. One is a strong J and the other a dominant P. The former organises his speeches well in advance and structures them in a logical and sequential manner. Very little is left to chance. This speaker plans exactly what he will say, the illustrations he will use, the humorous comments he will make, etc., and he follows his plan.

The second speaker is very different. He is a spontaneous person who prefers to "wing it". Being fully conversant with his subject matter, he briefly considers the content of his speeches and extemporises as he goes along. The illustrations he uses are not prepared in advance. Rather, his content is prompted by his knowing intuitively what to say when delivering his speeches.

Think about these two speakers and ask yourself, is one better than the other? The answer is "no"! Both are highly rated and outstanding; neither one is superior to the other; yet they are very different.

It is important to bear in mind that Psychological Type has nothing to do with skills, only predispositions or preferences.

Having said this, it should be remembered that the existence of dispositions means that certain things may come more easily to some Psychological Types than others. For example, the spontaneous, flexible person is likely to find it easier to adapt to sudden changes or unexpected occurrences than the more structured presenter.

Suppose the organised speaker (J) finds that, at a conference, a previous presenter had already addressed many of the issues he intended to raise; his thunder, so to speak, has been stolen. This speaker will probably find it more difficult to improvise and adapt his speech than the other, more flexible speaker (P). He is also more likely to be stressed by such unexpected events. Of course, in the end, our J speaker may do an outstanding job of accommodating, and even confirming, the validity of what his predecessor had to say, without the audience even knowing that he was temporarily thrown off balance. Yet, in truth, he would have experienced significant discomfort under such circumstances; far more than would the P speaker.

No type is, therefore, better than any other, though people of different types may have different responses and will be predisposed to behaving in different ways.

Can people change their Psychological Type?

The answer to this question is somewhat controversial.

On the one hand, most Jungian psychologists believe that one's type is genetically determined and relatively stable throughout life. On the other hand, some psychologists believe that human personality, including Psychological Type, is influenced more by one's environment and upbringing than by one's genes. Some point to the fact that if genetics were the determinant of personality then you would not get afflictions such as Multiple Personality Disorders (technically called Dissociated Identity Disorders or DID).

DIDs are conditions that are most often found in women who have been sexually abused or who have been repeatedly traumatised during childhood. To cope with their trauma they develop alter-egos, or diverse personalities, that take on separate, and often very different, characteristics. If we can acquire diverse personalities, some psychologists conclude that Psychological Type can be changed. After all, DID patients were not born with alter egos, they acquired them.

However, notwithstanding the debate about whether temperament can be changed, what is not in doubt is that everyone can develop skills to become a more rounded person. Thus "Perceiving" people are quite able to apply time-management and other techniques to better organise themselves. Then, with such skills, they may act as "Judging" people would, by intentionally structuring and managing themselves to achieve desired ends. This is in fact what type development is all about - deliberately acquiring those attributes that may not come spontaneously but are needed to be a more effective person.

We can illustrate this by taking the example of a good soccer player. Good players are able to kick the ball equally well with both right and left feet, but it does not come naturally. Players learn this important skill through diligent application. And, even when they are proficient with both feet, they will still have a preferred kicking foot.

So, too, it is with Psychological Type. People can acquire characteristics of other types but still retain their preferred tendencies. Thus, people do not usually change their type; rather, they are able to develop themselves by acquiring the strengths of other temperaments.

How universal are Psychological Types?

Although the tenets of Psychological Type were originally developed by Swiss psychiatrist, Carl Jung, and taken further by two American women, Katherine Briggs and Isabel Myers, Psychological Type has relevance throughout the world and not only in Europe and the USA. The reason is that the preferences measured are generic, and not culture-specific.

Substantiating the universality of Psychological Type is its widespread use in hundreds of countries throughout the world, from Japan to the USA, from the Northern Scandinavian countries to the Southern African Countries.

Are there individual differences between people of the same type?

Human nature is extremely diverse and its full extent cannot be gauged by any instrument. Thus Psychological Type, like any other form of assessment and classification of preferences, measures only a few of the range of possible characteristics.

Isabel Myers once said, "Every ESTJ is like every other ESTJ, like some other ESTJs and like no other ESTJ you have ever met". The same may be said of the other 15 Psychological Types. In other words, people who share the same preferences will show definite similarities, yet will still be highly individualistic in the way they behave, in what they choose to do, and in the values they hold.

Consider for example the following two people: Dr Joseph Hardie, a general surgeon, and Peter

Conradie, a plumber. Both are ISTJs and, in terms of their preferences, show similar traits (able to work for long periods on their own, systematic, highly conscientious, logical, analytical, well organised, and so on). They are both successful in their respective fields but, despite having the same Psychological Type, they are very different. One is a music lover, the other is tone deaf and does not care for music; one is happily married and a devoted husband and father, the other is a bachelor who has no interest in family life and does not intend getting married; one enjoys sports, the other prefers to read. These are just a few of the many differences that demonstrate the uniqueness of each individual despite the similarities in their preferences.

Does Psychological Type apply equally to men and women? Except for one of the four sets of dimensions, Psychological Type applies equally to both men and women with a 50-50 split in the E/I, S/N and J/P scales.

According to the Centre for Applications of Psychological Type, a research institution based in Gainesville, Florida (USA), the exception pertains to the T/F dimensions. On this scale there is a gender difference. Approximately two thirds of the female population score higher in F than T, whereas two thirds of males dominate in the T preference. This gender difference is consistent across cultures and has proved to be stable over the years.

Does the Psychological Type Inventory (or any other similar inventory) always reveal one's correct type?

Although most people will find that their type has been accurately determined by the Psychological Type Inventory (PTI) in this publication, some will find that it is not quite correct. In other words, one of the other 15 types better describes their preferences than the one indicated by the PTI. This is quite normal for the following reasons:

i.   no matter how valid and reliable the PTI, it is not perfect. There will always be a small percentage of people who get a reading that is not completely true to type;

ii.   some people may respond to certain questions in ways that reveal their wishes rather than their real attributes. This may happen either consciously or unconsciously; and

iii.   if only a slight preference is recorded on one or more scales, the respondent may need to check whether the alternative preference/s applies. The closer the scores within each pair of preferences, the less clear is the distinction between them.

It is important that, whatever inventory is used, respondents take responsibility for validating their own type.

How applicable is Psychological Type to children? Children begin to manifest their Psychological Type preferences in the first few years of their lives. By the time they get to school, most children will demonstrate a tendency towards one type or another. Although one cannot measure these preferences using the Psychological Type Inventory (it was designed for use by adults), there are other questionnaires that have been specifically developed for children. One of these is the Murphy-Meisgeier Type Indicator for children.

Can Psychological Type predict performance? The short answer to this question is a very definite "no"!

Psychological Type does not reveal skills. It cannot predict how well a person is likely to perform in any particular activity. Furthermore, Psychological Type does not determine potential.

However, what Psychological Type can predict is the comfort level of certain activities and how to accommodate activities that are outside one's natural predisposition. Let's take an example of two authors, one an Extrovert and the other an Introvert.

Writing books is, by its nature, a lonely pursuit. Authors spend long hours on their own, thinking through and clarifying ideas, plots or scenarios. They rewrite sentences many times to capture the essence of the message they wish to convey. Although one's writing skill is not revealed by Psychological Type, Extroverts will be drained by the long periods of isolation and contemplation whereas Introverts are likely to be stimulated by mental activities conducted in solitude.

A knowledge of type, while not predicting performance, can reveal factors that may influence the way in which people do things. Thus an Extrovert may want to punctuate relatively short bursts of writing with activities involving people, whereas an Introverted author may be quite happy to spend long hours alone.

How can knowledge of Psychological Type enhance working relationships and effective-ness? Those with little or no understanding of Psychological Type tend to believe that others should be motivated by the same things that interest them, and that people should behave in ways that are consistent with their view of what is appropriate.

Thus Extroverts are active people who speak their minds openly and have many friends. They are inclined to criticise Introverts, whom they see as quiet, reserved people who spend a great deal of time thinking and relatively little time acting. Introverts, on the other hand, tend to regard Extroverts as shallow people who think with their mouths and act impulsively. These two positions, accompanied by a critical attitude, could breed intolerance.

The same situation exists in the opposites of all dimensions, since each has its own particular preferences that are quite different from its counterpart. For example, practical Ss may see Ns as very conceptual with their heads in the clouds, whereas Ns could see Ss as lacking creativity and resistant to change. Ts may perceive Fs as illogical and easily swayed, while Fs could regard Ts as cold and impersonal. Js might think of Ps as disorganised people who are inclined to procrastinate, whereas Ps may consider Js to be inflexible and impatient.

Knowledge of Psychological Type enables one to recognise the diverse ways that people perceive things and respond to situations. With this knowledge comes an awareness that people have very different ways of experiencing the world. Furthermore, these differences are neither inferior nor superior. Rather, they provide a wonderful range of responses that engage different facets of personality. One way in which Psychological Type affects working relationships is that it promotes understanding instead of criticism and judgement.

Another way in which knowing Psychological Type may be used to enhance relationships is that it enables people to support one another from their strengths so that, together, they are able to be more effective than they would be individually.

To illustrate, suppose an ISTJ and an ENTP are required to work together. These two Psychological Types are very different, each with their strengths and weaknesses. In coming together, however, the strengths of one may compensate for the weaknesses of the other. By collaborating with each other from a position of understanding, and applying their natural preferences, the results will be far better than those achieved by two people of the same type who do not compensate for each other's weaknesses.

Whenever two or more people of the same type work together they will share significant strengths. There is the danger, however, that their common weaknesses may cause serious problems. So, if two ENFPs are working together without a knowledge of Psychological Type, their extroverted energy, creativity, sensitivity and flexibility will not ordinarily be balanced by a practical administrative capability whereby plans are thoughtfully developed and projects completed in an organised manner.

However, people who know about Psychological Type may choose to deliberately apply themselves to become more structured and detail-oriented in the work situation. Alternatively, they may choose to stick to their preferences and get the support of other, more administrative people.

Psychological Type, therefore, enables people to understand one another, support one another, build on one another's strengths, and accommodate one another's weaknesses in a spirit of co-operation and goodwill.

What are the downsides of categorising people according to type? The greatest danger of typecasting people is the notion that everybody of the same type demonstrates the same characteristics in every way. This is simply not so. Everybody is a unique individual and Psychological Type measures only a few of the many thousands of preferences that distinguish one person from another.

Even within the same sets of preferences, people are rated from a slight preference to a strong one, with significant variances between these extremes.

Another common problem encountered by people who misunderstand type is confusing preferences with skills. Psychological Type does not indicate how well a person is able to perform. An individual's skills are the result of dedicated application. They have little to do with temperament or type.

Generally speaking, if one regards type as a method of understanding oneself and others in four key areas (source of energy, information-gathering, decision-making and preferred lifestyle), and if one uses this information in ways that are beneficial and respectful, the proper use of type has no downside.

Is there any similarity between type and sun signs? Psychological Type is a relatively new discipline that comes from observing people in all walks of life, drawing conclusions from these observations, and using scientific research to validate these conclusions. It is thus based on research.

Sun signs come from the very old practice of attributing human nature to planetary interactions. As far as I am aware, they are not grounded in scientific research. This is not to say that sun signs are invalid. Rather, their origins and conclusions emanate from different sources. Thus there is little similarity between sun signs and type, other than that they both endeavour to throw some light on things people want to know about themselves and their fellow humans.

Conclusion

In my concluding comments about Psychological Type, I want to emphasise what this well-known, scientifically-based typology is, and what it is not.

Psychological Type is a reliable and valid system for identifying preferences in eight human categories. The inventories used to appraise these preferences are not tests; tests suggest that the higher you score the 'better' you are. Clearly this is not the case with type, where there is no better or worse, right or wrong.

This is an essential distinction to make. People who use Psychological Type to put people in boxes, predict capabilities or, in any way, suggest that some types are superior to others, are misusing this valuable aid.

It is also important to remember that Psychological Type does not measure anything about a person's beliefs, past experience, maturity, intelligence, stress levels, aspirations, or education, all of which significantly influence the way people behave.

What Psychological Type does measure are preferences on four, bi-polar scales (or eight categories) that cover major areas of life. Knowledge of where a person stands in these areas will enable an individual to understand his or her natural inclinations as well as those of other people. This knowledge can then be used to develop oneself, to accept oneself, to accommodate and relate to others, and to respect the differences that exist between people.